Famous Buildings
of
Frank Lloyd Wright

Bruce LaFontaine

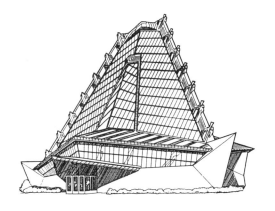

DOVER PUBLICATIONS, INC.
Mineola, New York

Bibliographical Note

Famous Buildings of Frank Lloyd Wright is a new work, first published by Dover Publications, Inc., in 1996.

DOVER *Pictorial Archive* SERIES

International Standard Book Number: 0-486-29362-9

Manufactured in the United States of America
Dover Publications, Inc., 31 East 2nd Street, Mineola, N.Y. 11501

INTRODUCTION

"Not only do I fully intend to become the greatest architect who has yet lived, but fully intend to be the greatest architect who will ever live. Yes, I intend to be the greatest architect of all time."
Frank Lloyd Wright

As boastful and immodest as the above statement might seem, many architects and art historians would agree that Frank Lloyd Wright achieved his goal. His work erupted onto the turn-of-the-century architectural scene like some powerful elemental force, with a clarity of vision that had practically no connection with previous forms of architecture. During his seven decades of professional practice, Wright inspired and amazed both the general public and the architectural world with his original, beautiful and daring buildings.

Frank Lloyd Wright was born on June 8, 1867, at Richland Center, Wisconsin. It is said that his mother knew from the start that her son would become an architect, and that she covered the walls of his nursery with pictures of architecture to encourage him in this pursuit. Wright's only formal architectural training came from the University of Wisconsin's civil engineering program; after one year of study, he left for Chicago to begin his professional career and was soon taken on by the prestigious firm of Adler & Sullivan, quickly becoming one of their master draftsmen. By the time Wright left to open his own practice in Oak Park, Illinois, he had already developed the technical ability and the sense of vision and purpose that would mark his work throughout his career.

As with the so-called Prairie houses which were his first projects, all of Wright's designs stemmed from his belief that a structure should be in harmony with its natural surroundings (such as the long, low vistas of the prairies, in the case of his first buildings). Wright felt that this unity between the structure and the landscape, as well as between the structure and the building materials and between the structure and its occupants, was at the core of what he called "organic architecture." Al-

though his architectural styles would change over the years, this central belief never wavered, and its expression can be found in his commercial, public and residential buildings alike.

Wright left his Oak Park practice in 1909 for a year of travel in Europe. He returned in 1911 and began what would become a continual process of designing and building his two great residences: Taliesin East, in Spring Green, Wisconsin, and Taliesin West, in Scottsdale, Arizona. These two very different landscapes, along with the constant process of redesigning and remodeling, continued to stir Wright's creativity, and the two homes reflect the developments and changing ideas in his work that came as the years passed.

Wright designed a total of more than one thousand buildings, over six hundred of which were constructed. Those of his buildings reproduced in this book—from the earliest residences, to his own homes and studios at Taliesins East and West, to the Beth Sholom Synagogue and the Guggenheim Museum—demonstrate his ability to combine the classical knowledge of the engineer with the romantic vision of the artist. It is said that every century is allotted only a few men or women of real genius; Frank Lloyd Wright may or may not be considered "the greatest architect of all time," but he was, most certainly, a true genius of the twentieth century.

NOTE: The illustrations in this book are placed in the approximate order in which the buildings were designed and constructed. Wright often worked on many designs at once: whatever lapse there may be in strict chronological order is due to the difficulty in defining the exact date of both the conception and the completion of each project.

William H. Winslow Residence (1893–1894), River Forest, Illinois.

"The machine is a marvelous simplifier; the emancipation of the creative mind, and in time, the regenerator of the creative conscience." —FLLW   Frank Lloyd Wright believed strongly in the idea of the machine as an "aesthetic tool" of the artist. He incorporated new technology and efficient production methods as an inherent element in his many design works. The coming of the twentieth century would see Wright exploit the "machine aesthetic" to full advantage.

This concept is illustrated by the two-story, brick and terra-cotta tile Winslow home, Wright's first commission as an independent practicing architect. It marks the beginning of several of his well-known design characteristics. The generous overhang of the roof eaves, for

instance, was to become a distinctive feature in many of Wright's residential projects, as was the use of horizontal bands of color or texture to separate the building into different levels. In the Winslow residence, the stone base is white; the brick first floor, yellow-brown; and the decorative tile work on the second floor, a rich, dark brown. The terra-cotta (clay) tiles were molded with a decorative pattern impressed into them. Many of the ornamental features on Wright's buildings, both exterior and interior, utilized nature themes. He used the patterns of trees, leaves, flower blossoms, seedpods and other natural forms as a basis to create an abstracted, stylized **design element.**

Frank Lloyd Wright House and Studio (1889–1909), Oak Park, Illinois. *"A house, I like to believe, is in status quo a noble consort to man and the trees. Therefore the house should have such repose and such texture as will quiet the world and make it graciously at one with external nature."* —FLLW   Wright began his independent practice in a studio attached to his wood-shingle and brick house, located in the Chicago suburb of Oak Park. He designed, built and lived in the structure from 1889 to 1909, continually modifying and rebuilding as he saw fit. He referred to its design style as "Seaside Colonial."

The exterior features a white stone base, with walls of multiple-hued brick and dark-stained wood shingles. The windows are leaded glass, with the interior illuminated by direct light from glass ceiling globes, which Wright nicknamed "sunlight," as well as by indirect grille lighting, which he called "moonlight." The manipulation of light and space was to become an important element in Wright's future work.

Frank Lloyd Wright House and Studio, fireplace alcove.   The interior walls are of unpainted wood and plaster, with natural wood used for details, fixtures and floors. Wright also designed the furniture for this house, as he did for many of his residential and commercial projects. Among his numerous interior creations were high slat-back chairs, end tables, hassocks, built-in bookcases and cabinets, and designed fabric pieces used as either wall hangings or throw rugs. The house's arched brick fireplace is located in an alcove off the living room. Over the mantel are wood panels with carved inscriptions expressing Wright's thoughts and values. This practice of displaying favorite quotations, mottoes and slogans was popular with Wright, and he made use of it quite often in his later work.

Ward W. Willits Residence (1901–1903), Highland Park, Illinois. Wright's architectural practice flourished during the years that he worked in his Oak Park studio. He was able to take on a large number of clients, primarily from the upper-class businessmen and professionals in the Chicago area, such as Ward W. Willits. The exterior of the Willits house uses light, sand-textured stucco (external plastering) to contrast with the dark wood trim, a method employed in many of Wright's early projects. He used the lines created by the dark wood as a directed visual rhythm, which he referred to as "eye music."

Instead of dividing the interior of the house into numerous smaller rooms by constructing walls, Wright chose to divide large rooms with screens and grilles made of wood, glass, metal, fabric or stone. These created "spatial areas" such as the living room, dining area or fireplace alcove. Wright considered the fireplace an important feature of residential architec-ture, and many of his most famous works were designed around a prominent fireplace.

With the Willits house and others built during this period, Wright began to use the design elements that would become well known as his "Grand Prairie School" of architecture. Primarily recognized for extended floor plans accentuating horizontal lines and with roof eaves extending well beyond the walls, this style is uniquely Wright's. It had its roots in Wright's Midwestern upbringing on the wide-open, flat expanse of prairie grasslands. He felt strongly that this long, low profile connected the structure to the land in a much more appropriate way than conventional styles. It echoed his feeling that a building should complement and harmonize with its natural surroundings, a principle that he maintained throughout his architectural practice.

William Fricke Residence (1901–1902), Oak Park, Illinois. Although the Fricke residence features some elements of Wright's famous "Grand Prairie School," it contradicts one of the primary characteristics of that style by accentuating the vertical instead of the horizontal. This may be evidence that, during this fairly early period in his career, Wright was partially influenced by popular turn-of-the-century European architecture.

The Fricke house features an exterior of light-colored stucco, with dark wood bands dividing the various levels and directing the eye upward. Its design also includes a three-story-high panel of leaded-glass windows facing the street. Although the house is situated quite close to the sidewalk and street, a level of privacy was maintained by building its stone base on a raised terrace of land several feet above the street level.

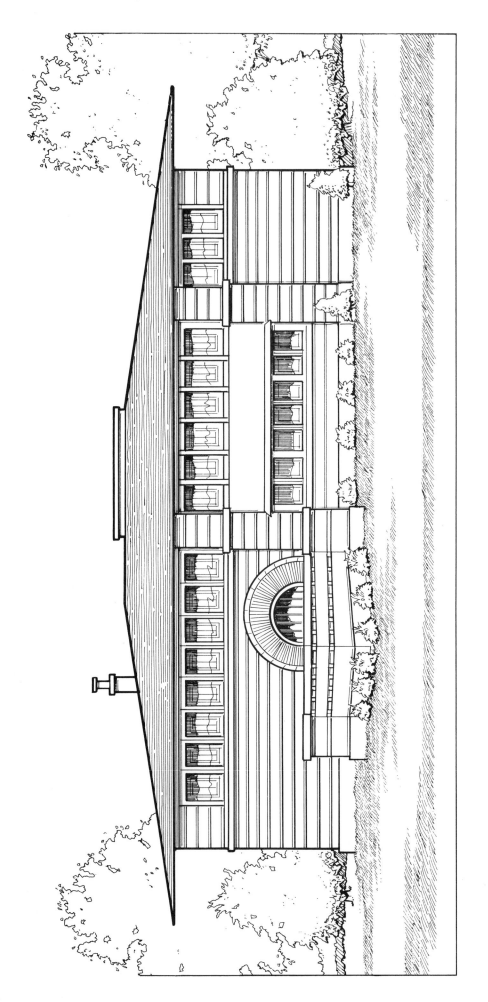

Arthur Heurtley Residence (1902), Oak Park, Illinois. *"Nothing remarkable about a brick, is there? A brick is a brick so far as most people are concerned. And it is not a very beautiful thing, is it? But what you can do with it!"*—FLLW   Another distinctive Wright design is the formidable brick structure he built for one of his Oak Park clients, Arthur Heurtley. It presents a massive, fortress-like façade to the world. Elevated several feet on its concrete "stylobate," or base, the house's exterior features a ground floor of alternating bands of brick: "courses" or rows of brick that alternate in color—dark red to rose pink—as well as in surface texture: one band projects out from the wall surface and the next remains flat and even with the surface. The second floor is marked by a long row of leaded-glass windows running almost the full length of the house. The eye-catching sunburst design of the arched brick entranceway is repeated around the living-room fireplace.

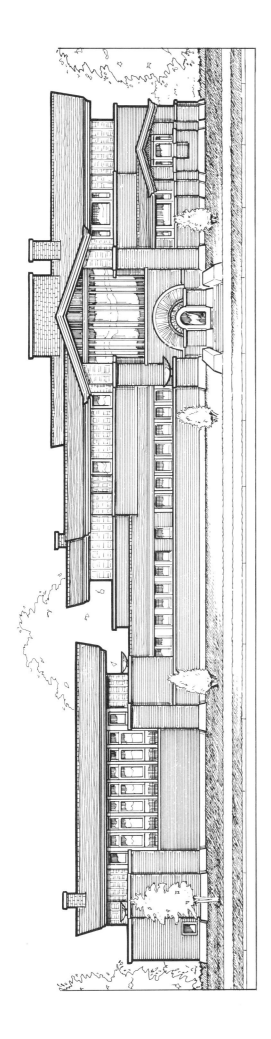

Susan Lawrence Dana Residence (1902–1904), Springfield, Illinois. One of Frank Lloyd Wright's recognized masterpieces is the impressive Susan Lawrence Dana residence. Incorporating many of the Prairie School design elements, the house stretches for over 300 feet on its street-facing side. It was built for Susan Lawrence Dana, a member of a prominent political and social family, who desired a structure spacious and grand enough to hold large social gatherings and entertain important persons. Its many rooms make use of alternating ceiling heights, from an intimate seven-foot level to a grand 24-foot reach.

The interior walls are of natural plaster, "scumbled" (roughly textured) and stained brown-gold, then sealed to prevent wallpapering (which Wright abhorred). The interior and exterior wood trim are of natural light oak. Wright designed the furniture for the house, as well as the lamps, tableware, linens, fixtures and rugs.

The exterior walls are of gray brick, with patterned stucco on the upper floors. The walls are broken up by horizontal and vertical bands of both clear leaded glass and intricately patterned stained glass. The house has been well preserved over the years and is now open to the public.

Susan Lawrence Dana Residence, interior front entranceway. *"I used to love sitting at my drawing board with T-square and triangle and concoct patterns for my windows. I evolved a whole language of my own in connection with these things."* —FLLW   The stained-glass windows in the Dana house are a product of Wright's affinity for straight, geometric, machine-cut glass design. The motif is based on an abstracted, stylized sumac leaf.

Larkin Company Administration Building (1903–1906), Buffalo, New York. *"The Larkin Building is not pretty; it is not intended to be. But it is not discordant and it is not false. It must stand or fall by its own merits, good or ill."* —FLLW Frank Lloyd Wright ventured into the larger world of commerical architecture with his design for the Larkin Building in Buffalo, New York. He secured this commission with the help of friend and admirer Darwin Martin, a Buffalo resident, for whom he later designed a large Prairie Style house.

Wright based his design on the principle that the workplace should be not a dark, dreary box with an uninspiring atmosphere, but a light, clean, airy environment that expresses the dignity of the individual and the democracy of labor.

Because the building site for this mail-order firm was located in an unattractive industrial area, Wright chose to wall off the external world and turn the focus of the building inward. To do this he designed an air-conditioning system and a massive skylight over a central atrium court. This open court ran the whole length of the building and was planted to create a gardenlike setting. Around the atrium court on each level of the building's six stories were offices with balconies, and terraces containing more greenery. The building also contained a rooftop restaurant, lounges, recreation rooms and a library for the employees' use.

Placed at various locations throughout the structure were plaques and signs presenting favorite Wright quotations on creativity, cooperation, productivity, diligence and other values he thought were appropriate for the workplace.

Considered a landmark design for commercial architecture, the Larkin Building became an unfortunate victim of urban renewal when it was torn down in 1950.

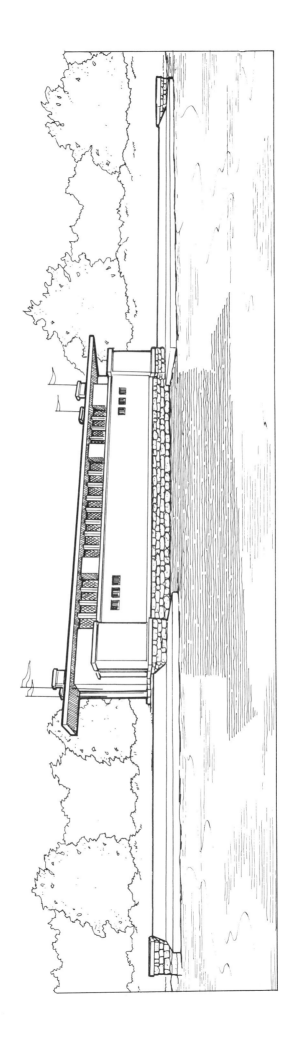

Yahara Boat Club Boathouse (1905), Madison, Wisconsin. Pictured above is a design that Wright created for a boathouse on the Yahara River, near Madison, Wisconsin. It was to be built of stucco, wood and stone and feature a shelter for the multi-man rowing shells on the ground floor, with floating platforms at both ends to launch the boats. The floor above the storage room was to contain a club meeting room and lockers. Although the boathouse never progressed beyond the drawing stage, it is an interesting example of the Wright Prairie design style applied to a nonresidential building.

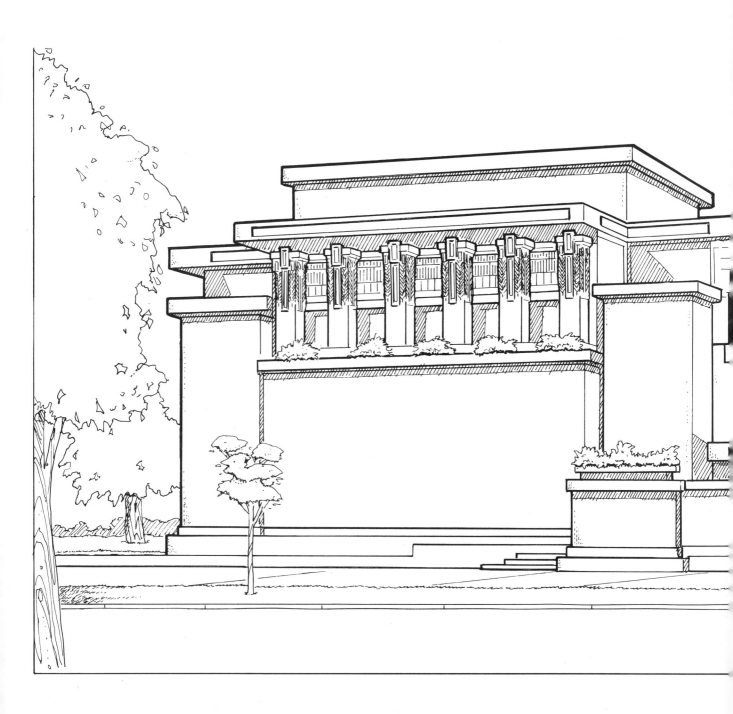

Unity Temple (1905–1908), Oak Park, Illinois. *"I often thought what a blessing this would have been for us if the Greeks would have had this steel, concrete, plate glass. If they had steel and glass, we wouldn't be thinking about this now; they would have done it for us."* —FLLW   Wright's first involvement with religious architecture was the innovative and daring Unity Temple, designed and built for the Unitarian congregation of Oak Park. It was like no other church or temple of the day.

The steel-reinforced concrete slabs and columns that form the church are organized into a double-cube arrangement. The larger

OR THE WORSHIP OF GOD
ND THE SERVICE OF MA

cube is the main worship hall and features a massive overhead skylight. The smaller cube is used for social activity and offices. The two cubes are connected by a low vestibule containing the main entranceway. In addition to the skylight, interior illumination is provided by both spherical and cube-shaped glass lamps.

The unconventional design of Unity Temple was met with mixed reviews by both its congregation and the public at large, but it was a resounding success in the architectural world. Wright's bold and unique vision provided impetus for other architects to venture into new areas of design for churches and temples.

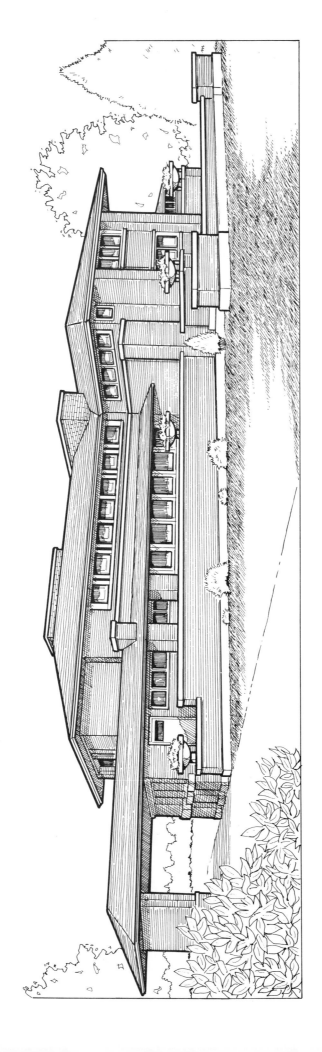

Darwin Martin Residence (1904–1906), Buffalo, New York.

"Art will reign as long as life and greater than ever her prestige will be when the harmony between commerce, science, and art is better understood." —FLLW

Built around the same time as the Larkin Building, the Martin residence is an excellent example of the Prairie Style house. Martin was a friend and business associate of the architect.

The masonry exterior is constructed of golden-brown brick, with darker bricks randomly interspersed throughout the courses. The long rows of first- and second-story windows are framed in copper. They include both leaded and stained-glass windows, including one of Wright's most famous designs, the "Tree of Life" motif. Placed at numerous points around the house perimeter are large urns for flowering plants.

Wright visited the upstate New York area quite often in connection with the Larkin Building, the several Buffalo area homes he designed and a well-known Prairie house he built in Rochester, the Edward E. Boynton residence.

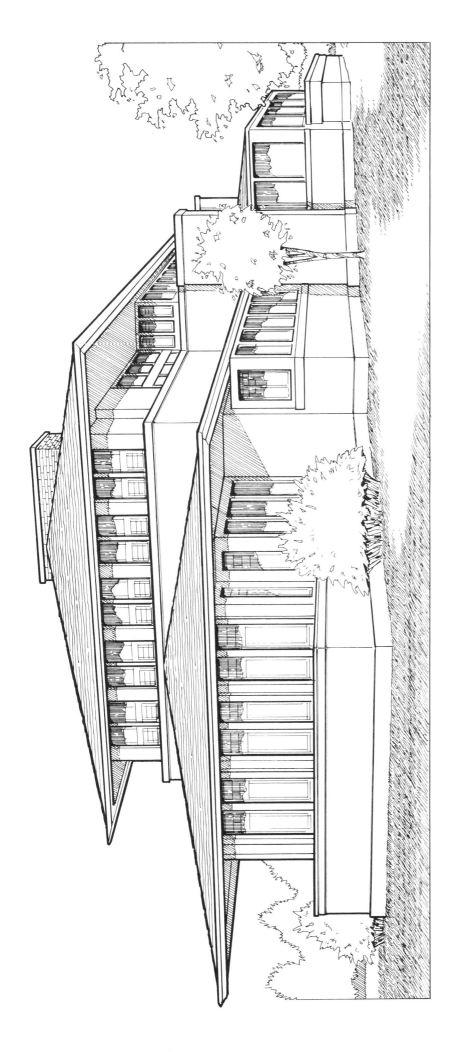

Edward E. Boynton Residence (1908), Rochester, New York. *"In architecture every-thing that is forward-looking and prophetic is in danger at the time in which it was built, and there are no exceptions to that rule."* —FLLW   The Boynton residence was built for widower Edward E. Boynton and his daughter Beulah, who lived in that area of Rochester known as the "Ruffled Shirt District." Looking like nothing else around it, the Boynton house is surrounded by stately residences in the Colonial, Georgian and Tudor styles. Unlike its neighbors, the structure is built of light stucco with a dark wood trim. The entranceway is located halfway down one side of the house and opens into a reception area, which in turn leads to a large living room, dining room and den area. These areas are separated by screens and grilles, but all share a large expanse of stained-glass windows. The house also features the use of long, narrow clerestory windows for additional light. This type of window is located high on the wall just below the ceiling. Wright also designed the interior furnishings.

Although this was one of his smaller Prairie houses, Wright gave it much attention during the construction process. He visited the site numerous times, making the long journey from Oak Park by train, and often sleeping in the partially completed structure under a makeshift canvas tent.

15

Frederick C. Robie Residence (1909–1910), Chicago, Illinois. *"The house became known in Germany as 'dampfer' (ocean-liner) architecture. It was a good example of a prairie house of that period. This further emphasized that the machine could be a tool in the hands of the artist."* —FLLW   The Robie house represents the epitome of Frank Lloyd Wright's Prairie Style of architecture. With its sleek, low-slung and streamlined appearance, it had a powerful impact on American and European architecture of the day. It was referred to as the "house of the Machine Age."

The structure was built for Frederick C. Robie, a Chicago engineer and admirer of Wright's work. The exterior walls are of brown brick with white stone trim. The front facade features rows of leaded and stained-glass windows, all with Wright's nature-based, stylized geometric patterns. The great sweep of roof overhang is accomplished by means of cantilevers.

Using brick, stone, concrete, steel and glass, Wright was able to sculpt a strong, dynamic composition of forms with great artistic sensitivity. Almost demolished several times, this most famous example of Wright's Prairie architecture is now well preserved and protected as a National Landmark.

Frederick C. Robie Residence, living room. The first-floor interior of the Robie house is almost one long, uninterrupted living room/dining area, broken up only by the central staircase to the second floor. Wright designed all of the furniture and interior fixtures to be made from wood and bronze, including high slat-back chairs, coffee tables, and tables, sofas and lamps.

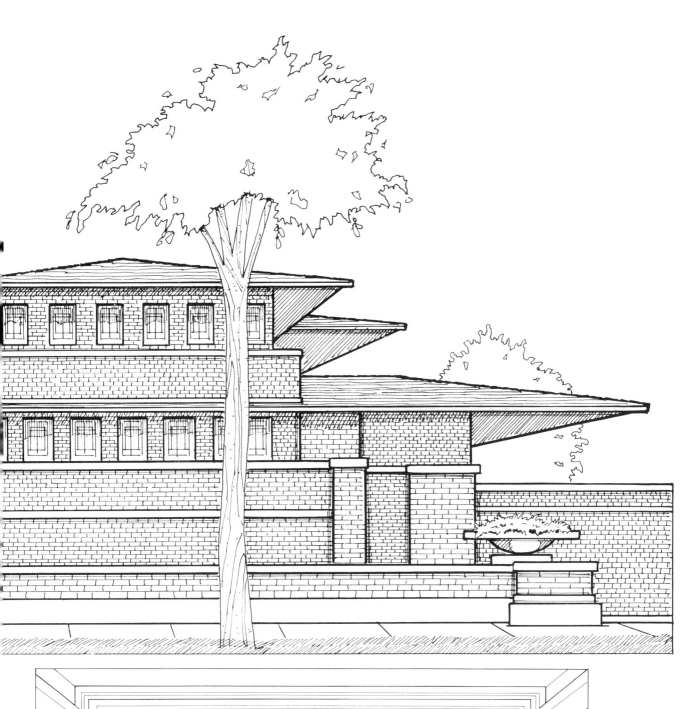

Mrs. Thomas H. Gale Residence (1909), Oak Park, Illinois. One of the last of Wright's Prairie Style houses to be built in his Oak Park neighborhood was the two-story Gale house. A fairly simple structure of light stucco and dark wood, it incorporates a concept followed by Wright for the use of cantilever construction in residential architecture. This idea eventually led him to his world-famous house design, "Fallingwater."

A cantilever is simply a beam or platform that projects out from the main body of a structure, held in place only by a counterweight on the near end. The Gale house demonstrates this with its generous flat roof overhang and its projecting second-story terrace/balcony.

Midway Gardens, (1913–1914), Chicago, Illinois, entrance gate. *"I clearly saw my trusty T-square and aspiring triangle as means to the Midway Gardens end I had in view. Its forms could be made into a festival for the eyes no less than music made festival for the ears, I knew. And this could all be genuine building, not scene painting."* —FLLW   In 1913 Frank Lloyd Wright began the most ambitious architectural project he had yet attempted—an extensive outdoor entertainment center. Wright's interest in this project was sparked by his experience during the year-long visit he made to Germany in 1909, for he had been impressed by the atmosphere and social culture he had seen at the outdoor beer gardens there.

Wright felt that his vision for the Midway Gardens of Chicago could be an architectural showcase for dining, drinking and dancing. He would design the entire project, including all the interior appointments, furnishings, carpets, tableware, lamps, linens, murals and sculptures. The center would also contain an indoor restaurant and dance floor for colder weather.

Occupying one square block of land along Chicago's Cottage Grove Avenue, Midway Gardens was constructed of brick, stone and reinforced concrete. Wright also used cast concrete for the many sculptural figures and ornamental details that he included in the design. Shown above is one of the Gardens' "festival for the eyes" entrance gates.

Wright's design for the Gardens also included exhibit areas for artwork by the newly emerging modern painters and sculptors. His desire was to intermingle and display together at one site as many of the arts as possible.

When it opened in 1913, Midway Gardens was a popular and critical success. Unfortunately, because of poor management by the original financial backers, the project went bankrupt after just two years. It was then sold to a beer company that made many changes to Wright's original concept and allowed the structure to fall into disrepair, until it was finally demolished in 1929.

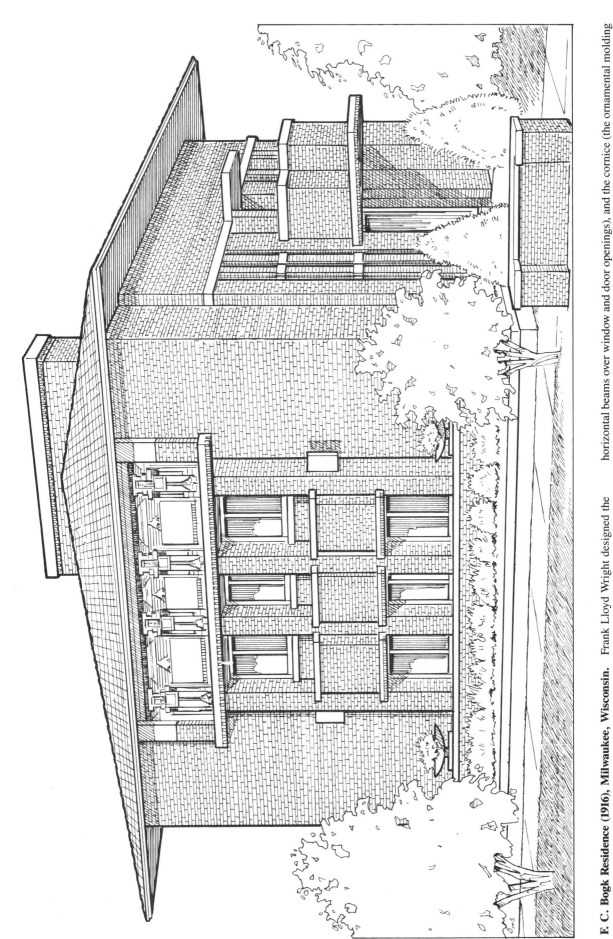

F. C. Bogk Residence (1916), Milwaukee, Wisconsin. Frank Lloyd Wright designed the Bogk residence during the five-year period when he was working on the Imperial Hotel project in Tokyo, Japan. Some elements of the hotel design can be seen in the Bogk house, especially on the front facade.

The structure is built of brown-yellow bricks, with cast concrete used for the lintels (the horizontal beams over window and door openings), and the cornice (the ornamental molding running along the wall just below the roof). The cornice design is a stylized Assyrian architectural theme.

The "art-glass" (leaded or stained-glass) window pattern is a fairly simple geometric one, and, as was his usual practice, Wright designed all the interior furnishings.

Imperial Hotel (1916–1922), Tokyo, Japan, view from Imperial courtyard.   "*The Imperial Hotel is designed as a system of gardens and sunken gardens and terraced gardens . . . of balconies that are gardens and loggias that are also gardens . . . and roofs that are gardens . . . until the whole arrangement becomes an interpretation of gardens. Japan is a garden-land.*" —FLLW   Frank Lloyd Wright's significant collection of Japanese prints and bronze sculptures spurred in him an interest in visiting Japan. In 1916 he traveled to Tokyo with the hope of designing a building there. The Japanese were very impressed with his work and reputation, and he was awarded a contract to build a large hotel across from the Imperial Palace.

Wright was given two overriding requirements for the hotel design: first, that the building should be as earthquake-proof as possible, since earthquakes are frequent in Japan; and second, that the building should be in respectful harmony with the neighboring Imperial Palace. Wright was confident that he could create a building that combined a contemporary architectural design with a traditional Japanese look.

The overall design of the hotel was H-shaped, with the central block for reception, offices and meeting rooms, and the two long wings for guest rooms and suites. The wings were separated from the central building by numerous terraces, ponds and bridges. The buildings themselves were constructed from reinforced concrete and brick.

A large part of the grounds and buildings was decorated with sculptures and ornaments hand carved from "oya" stone, a lava-based material. They embodied traditional Japanese themes and images and were situated along rooftops, decks, tops of columns and terraced walls. Wright again provided the design for all the carpets, textiles, furniture, tableware and linens.

The success of Wright's design was proved when the Imperial Hotel withstood the Great Earthquake of 1923, which ravaged much of Tokyo. The hotel was only destroyed in 1968 by being demolished to make way for another building.

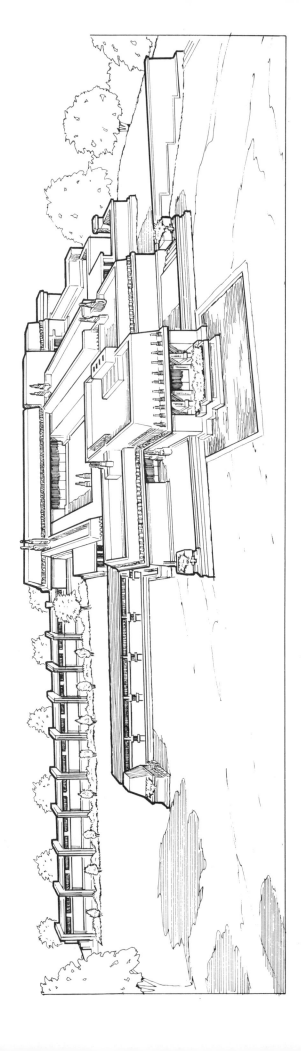

Aline Barnsdall Residence, "Hollyhock House" (1917–1922), Los Angeles, California.

"When organic architecture is properly carried out, no landscape is ever outraged by it but is always developed by it. The good building makes the landscape more beautiful than it was before the building was built." —FLLW   A new direction in Wright's architecture began in 1917 with the strikingly designed "Hollyhock House." It was created for Aline Barnsdall, a wealthy Los Angeles socialite and theater enthusiast, who wanted a complex of buildings devoted to experimental-theater production.

The main residence is built from cast concrete and ornamented with a decorative theme derived from the hollyhock, Ms. Barnsdall's favorite flower. The stylized floral design developed by Wright runs along the concrete parapets of the roofline and across the colonnades and planters, and is even found in the building's interior on the backs of chairs. The residence is built around a large enclosed courtyard, with the inside, courtyard-facing walls having a great expanse of glass windows and doors, but with very few windows on the outside walls.

A novel feature of Hollyhock House is a stream of water that runs from a large reflecting pool, alongside the dining-room windows, and then disappears, resurfacing inside the living room in a pool surrounding the fireplace. From there it continues outside to another reflecting pool. Above the fireplace Wright designed a mural representing an abstract interpretation of the four ancient elements: Fire, Water, Sky and Earth.

Aline Barnsdall lived in Hollyhock House for only a few years. She eventually moved to Europe and donated the house to the City of Los Angeles to be used as an artists' colony. It fell into disrepair at the hands of subsequent owners but is now in the process of restoration.

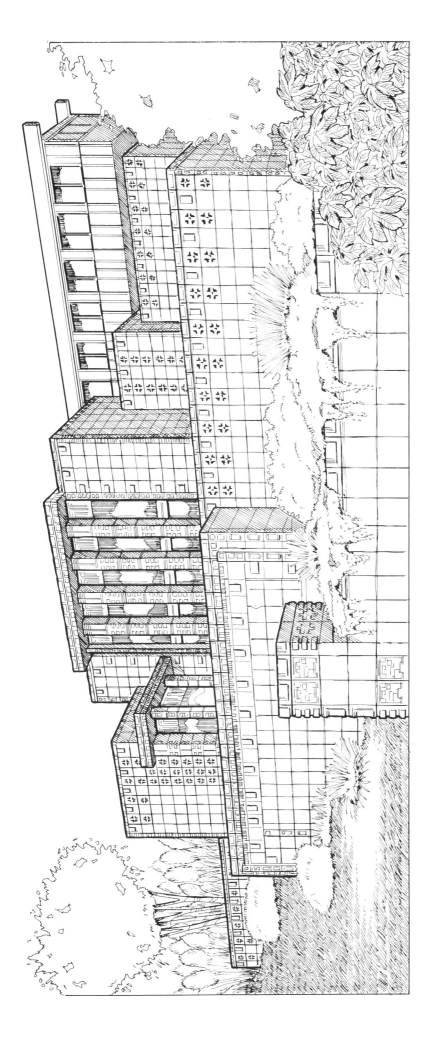

John C. Storer Residence (1923–1924), Hollywood, California. *"We would take that despised outcast of the building industry—the concrete block—out from under foot or from the gutter—find hitherto unsuspected soul in it—make it live as a thing of beauty—textured like trees. Yes, the building would be made of the 'blocks' as a kind of tree itself standing at home among the other trees in its own native land."* —FLLW   One of four Los Angeles-area houses using Wright's unique cast concrete-block design, the Storer residence exemplifies Wright's belief that the concrete block was more appropriate and natural to the Southern California setting than many of the other construction materials being used in the area at that time.

The blocks themselves were cast on the construction site using molds of varying pattern. Some blocks were solid and some had decorative perforations that were either left open or filled with glass. The blocks were strengthened and bonded together by steel rods inserted horizontally and vertically between the courses. The technique can be likened to weaving with steel and concrete, and it made for an extremely strong structure.

Wright considered his concrete-block houses successful as a new and innovative style for residential construction, but they were not popular with the public, whose preference was for more common "period"-style homes.

Taliesin East I, II, III (1911–1959), Spring Green, Wisconsin, exterior. *"I believe that the ideal of organic architecture forms the origin and source, the strength and fundamentality, the significance of everything ever worthy of the name Architecture."* — FLLW   The story of Frank Lloyd Wright's Wisconsin residence and studio, Taliesin, begins in 1911. Wright had decided to move his practice from Chicago to Spring Green, Wisconsin, a valley near his birthplace of Richland Center. Here, for a period of nearly fifty years, he would design and build, redesign and rebuild, his summer home and studio.

The name "Taliesin," in the Welsh language of Wright's ancestors, means "shining brow." Wright chose this name because he decided to build his home into the "brow" of the hillside, rather than on top of the hill. Taliesin was also the name of an ancient Welsh poet who celebrated the art and culture of the people of Wales in his work.

Taliesin I, begun in 1911, was badly damaged by a fire in 1914. Wright immediately began to rebuild Taliesin II from its remains, a project that occupied him from 1914 until 1925. Another fire in 1925 caused Wright to again redesign and rebuild the structure. From 1925 until his death in 1959, Wright was continually changing, adding on and reconstructing what we now call Taliesin III.

The complex is comprised of many structures—some connected, some separate—including the main residence for the family, rooms for the apprentices who were part of Wright's Taliesin Fellowship, the studio, drafting rooms and a theater. The buildings are constructed from brown-gray stone, wood and concrete.

The Taliesin Fellowship was an apprenticeship program for architectural students, who lived and worked with Wright and who comprised his professional staff. For the privilege of working with the Master Architect, the students paid a nominal fee and provided an inexpensive labor force for his many projects. Wright referred to the Taliesin Fellowship as "the fingers of my hand."

Taliesin III, interior drafting room.   Depicted here is the network of projecting wooden beams that support the roof of Taliesin's drafting room. Wright described their appearance as an "abstract forest." At one end of the drafting room is an enormous fireplace (not shown), large enough for a person to stand in. Above the fireplace is the carved inscription: "What a Man does, that he has."

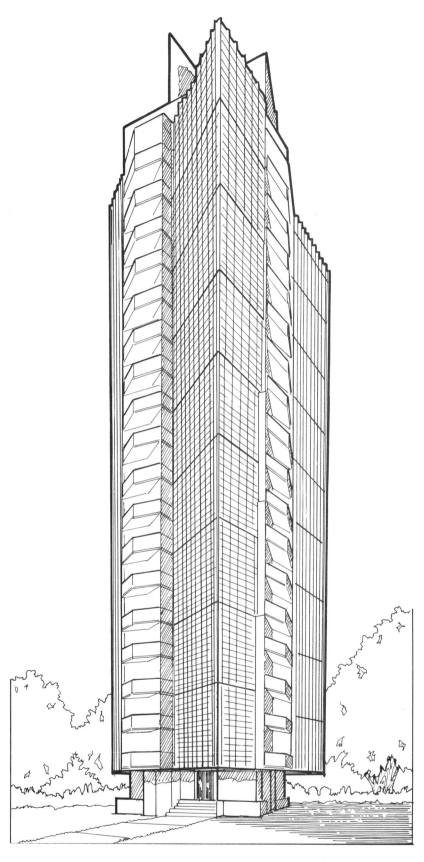

St. Mark's-in-the-Bouwerie Towers (1929), New York, New York.   The design for the St. Mark's Towers project called for a nineteen-story tower to be built using the cantilever principle. It would be constructed around a steel core, with each floor jutting out from the central shaft. Wright felt that this method would make a building that was one-third lighter and three times stronger than the conventional masonry-covered steel-skeleton building.

The Stock Market crash of 1929 and the Great Depression that followed prevented the St. Mark's Towers project from going forward. In 1953 Wright revised and updated the original plan, incorporating it into his only skyscraper to be constructed, the Price Company Tower.

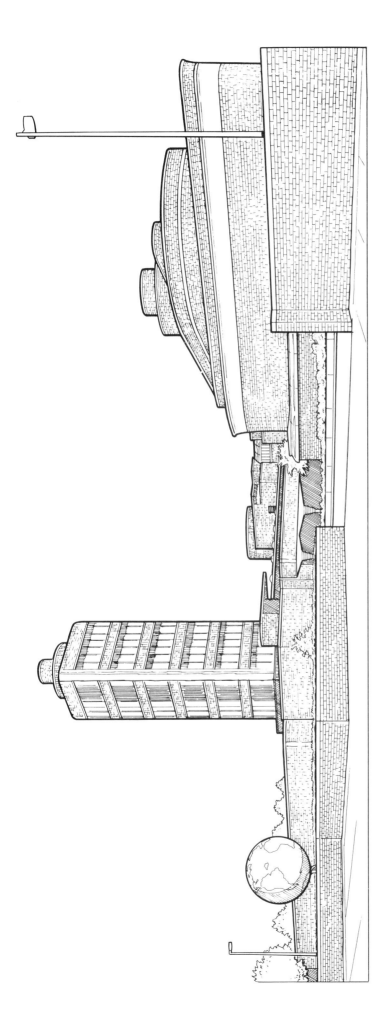

S. C. Johnson & Son Co. Administration Building and Research Tower (1936–1939 & 1944), Racine, Wisconsin. *"Organic architecture designed this great building to be as inspiring a place to work as any cathedral ever built was in which to worship. It was meant to be a socio-architectural interpretation of modern business at its top and best."* — FLLW   Perhaps the most widely admired example of Frank Lloyd Wright's commercial architecture, the Johnson Wax Building, as it is popularly known, was an enormous success for Wright both critically and with the general public. Some of the public acclaim may have been due to the timing of its construction; the project was finished in 1939, the same year as the hugely publicized and popular New York World's Fair. The design fit right into the Fair's theme of the promise of modern American technology and the wonders of the future that it would bring.

Primarily, however, the admiration for the building was due to Wright's own imaginative and unique vision. Distinctly streamlined in appearance, the buildings were situated in an unattractive industrial area. To counter this, Wright again used the strategy he employed for the Larkin Building, turning the focus of the design inward so as to "seal off" the outside environment.

Wright made great use of overhead light, employing both natural light and long, clear glass tubes that refract and diffuse light. Many of the inner office walls are made from similar translucent glass tubes and feature Wright-designed curvilinear metal and wood chairs, desks and other office furnishings.

The main work room is supported by a "forest" of 21-foot-tall concrete and steel columns. Smaller at the base than at the top, the columns spread into large circular "lily pads" at the ceiling level. They provide the support for the ceiling in contrast to a conventional structure, which uses the exterior walls for support. The exterior walls of the buildings are of warm red brick with a light stone trim. The Research Tower was built in 1944 and was connected to the main building by a tunnel having a glass-tube ceiling.

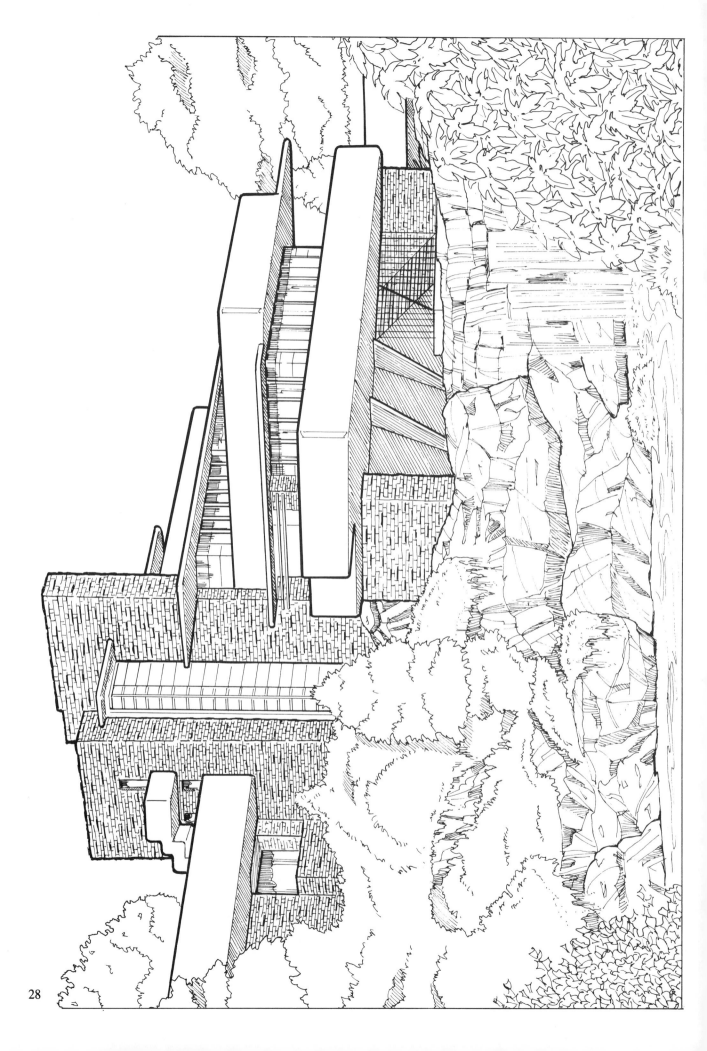

Edgar J. Kaufmann Residence, "Fallingwater" (1934–1937), Bear Run, Pennsylvania. *"The visit to the waterfall in the woods stays with me, and a domicile has taken vague shape in my mind to the music of the stream. When contours come, you will see it."*—FLLW   The Kaufmann residence, known as "Fallingwater," is without doubt the most famous and admired architectural work created by Frank Lloyd Wright, and it is perhaps the best-known example of modern American architecture.

Situated on a cliffside and projecting out over the edge of a waterfall, Fallingwater is the embodiment of Wright's concept of organic architecture. Built of concrete, stone and glass, the building features staggered terraces, cantilevered decks and alcoves, that all echo the look of the natural stone cliffside. Facing the stream and waterfall, a wall of windows invites the woodland environment inside.

Wright designed the house for Edgar J. Kaufmann, a Pittsburgh department-store magnate whose son had been an apprentice to Wright in the Taliesin Fellowship. What was meant to be a weekend retreat quickly became so famous an attraction that an additional guest house was built a short way up the hillside, connected to the main house by a walkway. Fallingwater and its surroundings have transcended mere architecture to become a symbol of an age, a culture and an artist.

Fallingwater, living room.   The interior of Fallingwater has natural stone walls and floors, with a large boulder embedded in front of the fireplace. The house was built around the boulder and was designed to use the rock as a counterweight for the cantilevered terrace that overlooks the waterfall.

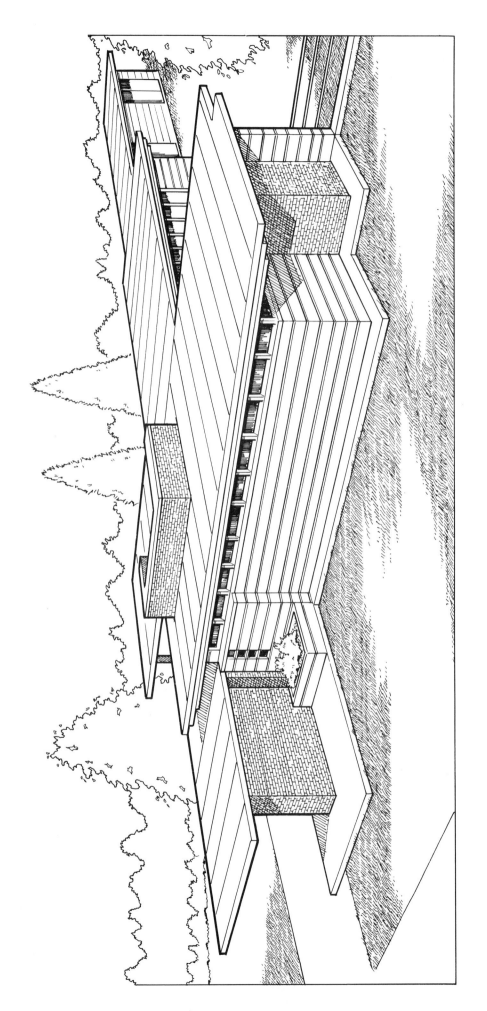

Herbert Jacobs' "Usonian House" (1936), Madison, Wisconsin. *"Form and Function are one."* —FLLW   Wright introduced a new concept in residential architecture with the advent of the "Usonian House." He developed a design for a house that was smaller and less expensive to construct than the average house had been, making it affordable to many more people.

Wright's goal was a construction cost of no more than $5000 and an architectural fee of just $500. The basic plan is L-shaped, with the living room in one wing and the bedrooms in the other; the kitchen is situated in the middle. The foundation is a concrete platform with heating pipes cast into the concrete. There is no basement—just a small area under the kitchen for the furnace.

The Herbert Jacobs residence was the first of many Usonian houses to be built. It features exterior walls of brick and horizontal wooden boards. The outside-facing walls have clerestory windows for privacy, while the walls facing the terrace and landscaped garden area feature full-length glass.

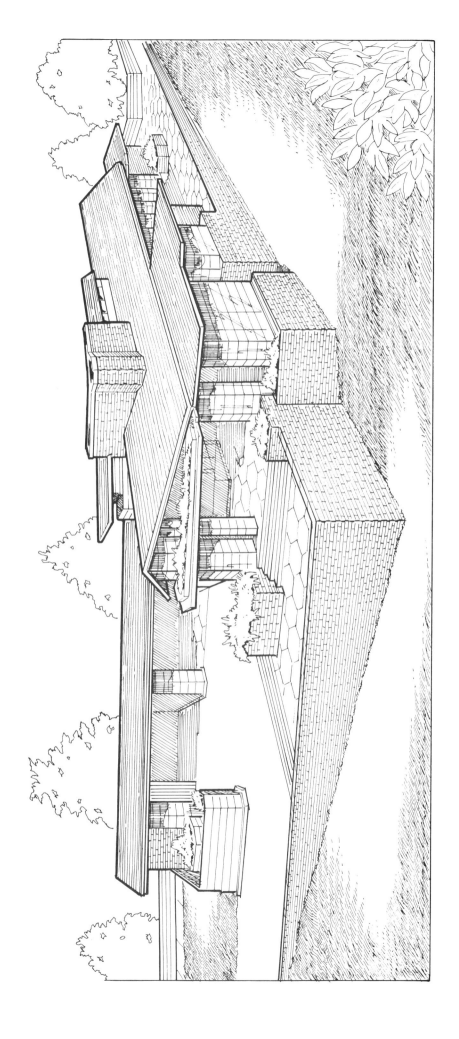

Paul R. Hanna Residence, "Honeycomb House" (1936–1937), **Stanford, California.**
"Human houses should not be like boxes, blazing in the sun—Any building for humane purposes should be an elemental, sympathetic feature of the ground, complementary to its nature and environment, in kinship with the terrain." —FLLW   Wright experimented with using the hexagon as a basic design theme in the Hanna residence, nicknamed "Honeycomb House" because its shape reflects that of an individual honeycomb cell. He felt that the 120- degree angles of the hexagon allowed for a more organic and flexible unit than the 90-degree angles of the square or rectangle.

The house used brick, glass and a wooden "board and batten" construction, a method in which narrow strips of wood are interspersed between wider wooden boards. Wright used this construction style for many of his Usonian houses.

Taliesin West (1937–1959), Scottsdale, Arizona. *"I am struck by the beauty of the desert, by the dry, clear, sun-drenched air, by the stark geometry of the mountains—the entire region was an inspiration in strong contrast to the lush, pastoral landscape of my native Wisconsin."*—FLLW   Taliesin West was Frank Lloyd Wright's large, rambling winter residence, studio and school for his Taliesin Fellowship apprentices, located in the Arizona desert just outside of Phoenix. Wright was attracted to this area after spending the winter in Arizona recovering from a bout of pneumonia. The site is located in the Paradise Valley at the foot of the McDowell Mountains.

The construction of Taliesin West began in 1937, when Wright was 70 years old, and it continued on for the next twenty-two years. The basic plan consisted of living quarters for Wright and his family, rooms for the apprentices, a large drafting/work room, a kitchen, music room, auditorium and Wright's private studio.

The buildings themselves were constructed from wood, concrete and stone. The exterior walls were made by pouring concrete into wooden forms, then placing desert "rubble rock" found at the site into the forms, with the flat sides of the rocks facing the inside of the forms. Surrounding the buildings are pools, fountains, several green gardens and a desert garden.

Wright's inspiration for the design came from the varied and contrasting shapes of the surrounding desert landscape, with its multihued hills and mountains, its canyons and rock formations. The whole concept for Taliesin West sprang from his appreciation for the stark, harsh beauty of the desert. Taliesin West was remodeled and rebuilt numerous times over the years, as Wright returned each year to escape the rugged Wisconsin winters, fresh and energetic with new ideas.

Taliesin West, view from the western end.   Many sections of the
roof of Taliesin West, including that of the main work room, were
made from large redwood beams, with white canvas stretched from
beam to beam. This provided a soft, diffused light within the area.
Over the years the canvas was replaced by a variety of more durable
materials. The roofs of other portions of Taliesin, such as the large
auditorium, were made of redwood or stone.

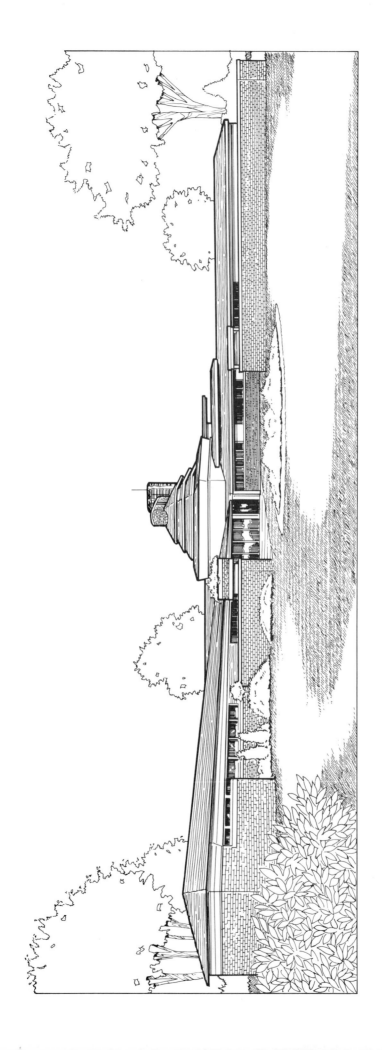

Herbert F. Johnson Residence, "Wingspread" (1937–1939), Wind Point, Wisconsin. One of Frank Lloyd Wright's largest and most ambitious residential designs, and one of the last of his great Prairie houses, "Wingspread" sprawls over the Wisconsin countryside. It was built for the president of S. C. Johnson & Son Company.

The structure is comprised of four wings emanating from a central three-story-high living room, called the "Great Hall." Rising above the living room and accessible from a series of spiral stairs is a glass tower or cupola that affords a magnificent view of the surrounding prairie plains. A total of five fireplaces are located around the massive central chimney.

Each of the outspread wings was designed with a specific purpose: one for the Johnson children's rooms, one for guest rooms, one for the kitchen and servants' quarters, and one, slightly upraised from the level of the others, for the master-bedroom suite. The overall structure, of warm brown-red brick, includes numerous overhead skylights.

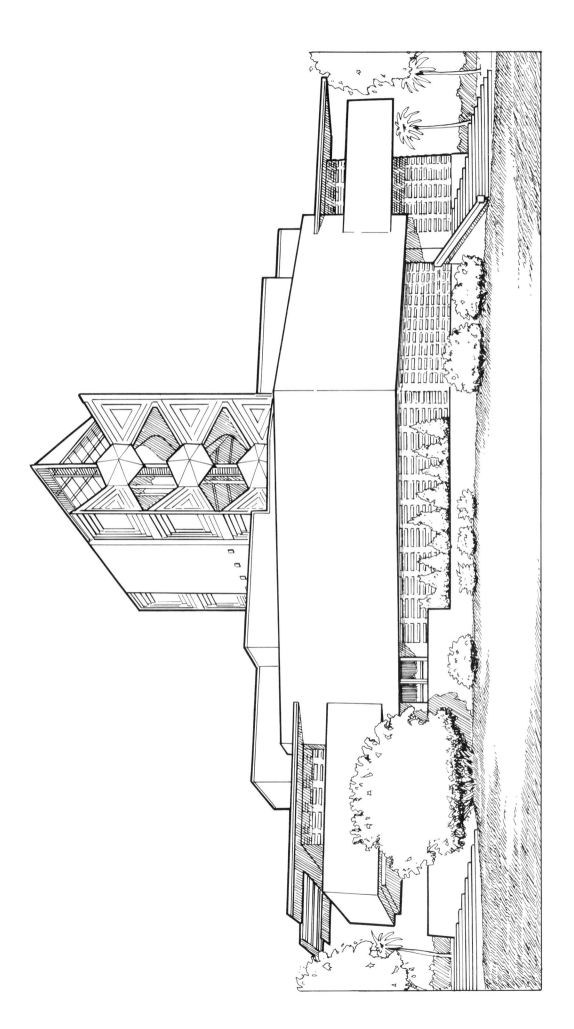

Annie Pfeiffer Memorial Chapel, Florida Southern College (1938), Lakeland, Florida. During the same period that Taliesin was beginning to take shape in Arizona, Wright undertook an ambitious project for the design of a new campus for Florida Southern College, a coeducational Methodist school.

The original plan called for a total of 13 buildings, with a central focus on the Chapel; only ten buildings were actually constructed. A primary design theme was the use of strong diagonal lines and forms, much as at Taliesin West. This can be seen quite clearly in the skeletal-steel chapel tower with its slanting glass skylights.

Many of the concrete blocks used in the construction were molded with patterns and perforations. Colored glass was embedded in the perforations to refract light into colorful "jewels." These multicolored spots of light enhance the inherent beauty of the white campus buildings set against the tropical green landscape and clear blue sky.

**C. Leigh Stevens Residence, "Auldbrass Plantation"
(1939–1941), Yemasee, South Carolina.** *"Wood, of course, is
the most friendly of materials. Nothing is so friendly to man as the
tree. And the tree is wood. Wood has certain qualities—certain
characteristics—and if you use it according to those characteristics
and are especially in love with them yourself, you'll come out with a
wooden structure that is really beautiful."* —FLLW   The Stevens
residence, nicknamed "Auldbrass Plantation," was built with a low
profile befitting the flat, wet grasslands of its location in South
Carolina. The house is constructed of brick and wood. Wright
designed the brick walls to rise vertically, while the wooden walls
were built with an inward slant. The house is one of a complex of
buildings that includes a guest house, caretaker's house, farm buildings, stable, barn and cabins for workers.

Since its construction in 1939, the house has fallen into a consider-
able state of disrepair. It was bought by a new owner in 1987,
however, and is currently undergoing careful restoration. This process is being done with the help of Wright's grandson Eric Lloyd
Wright.

C. Leigh Stevens Residence, living room. Wright's generous use of wood for the Stevens living room can be clearly seen in the illustration. He also used two bands of clerestory windows with warm-colored stained glass. These can be seen where the walls join the ceiling and again where the main support beam touches the ceiling.

Unitarian Church (1945–1951), Madison, Wisconsin. Many of Frank Lloyd Wright's most dramatic and powerful buildings are religious structures, as is demonstrated by his design for the Unitarian Church in Madison, Wisconsin. Wright's own family background was rooted in Welsh Unitarian theology and philosophy; one of the principal tenets of this religion is the belief in the "unity of all things," a belief that Wright strived to incorporate into his architecture.

The church is situated on a hillside sloping down to Lake Men-

dota. The dramatic "prow" of the main worship room faces the lake. The smaller building houses offices and meeting rooms. They are both constructed of native Wisconsin limestone, generous amounts of glass, and copper for the main roof.

In the main auditorium, a large limestone fireplace sits at one end, facing the dramatic triangular window wall at the other. Some visitors to the church see an implied shape of hands clasped in prayer in the powerful rise of the roofline.

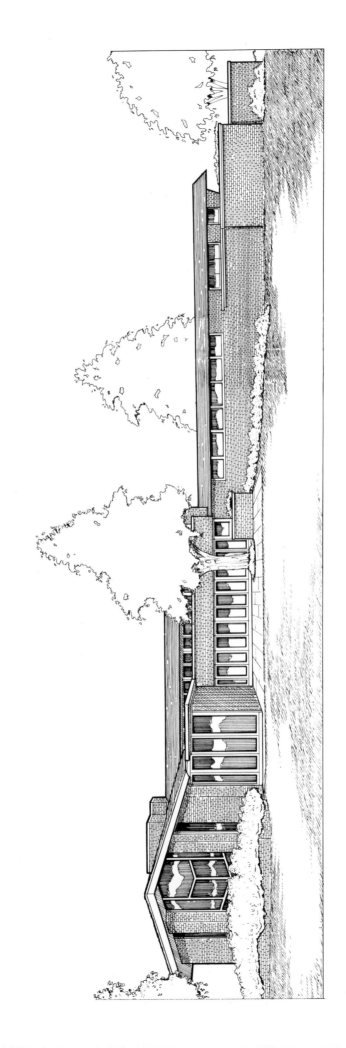

Herman T. Mossberg Residence (1948), South Bend, Indiana, view from the garden. The Mossberg house was built using a Usonian L-shaped plan that has been expanded to incorporate more rooms. The street-facing side presents an almost windowless wall of protective brick to the world for privacy. The garden side is built with multiple stories of glass walls and doors, designed to invite in the natural surroundings.

An interesting feature of the Mossberg house is the staircase to the upper floor. The stairs themselves are concrete slabs wrapped in carpeting. They are individually suspended from the ceiling rafters by steel rods of varying length. These rods also act as a handrail. Like many of Wright's residential projects, the Mossberg house features chairs, tables, hassocks and built-in cabinets and bookcases designed by the architect.

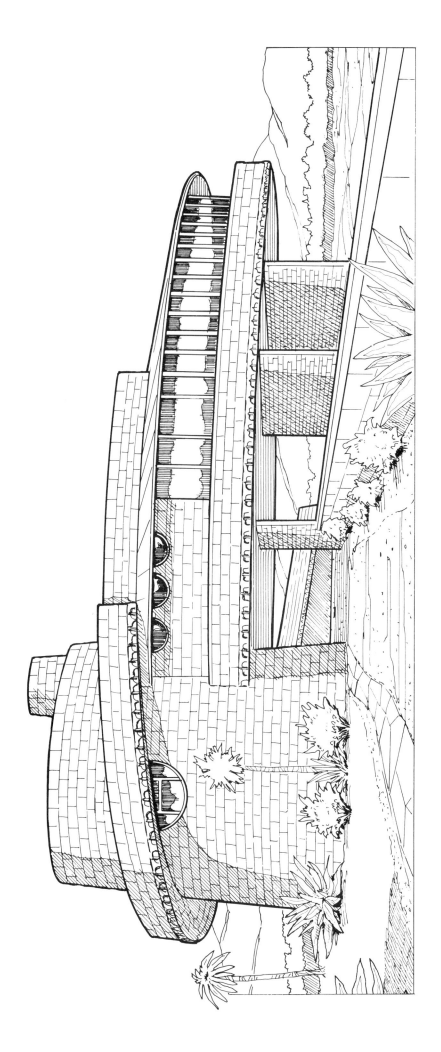

David Wright Residence (1950–1954), Phoenix, Arizona. This unique spiral house was designed by Wright in 1950 for his son David. It is set in the middle of a citrus grove, not far from Camelback Mountain in Phoenix, Arizona. Wright's design elevated the structure off the hot desert floor, thereby providing cool and shaded areas under the house for grass and shrubbery.

Since David Wright was in the concrete-block business, the elder Wright decided that concrete would be a natural material for the home's construction. The courses of blocks that form the house are staggered from one row to another to give a feeling of texture to the surface. The house describes a complete circle, its elevation spiraling upward on seven progressively higher concrete pylons.

The rooms run off the curl of the building, ending with the master bedroom and its cantilevered terrace. The interior ceilings are of mahogany, and the roof itself is made of metal.

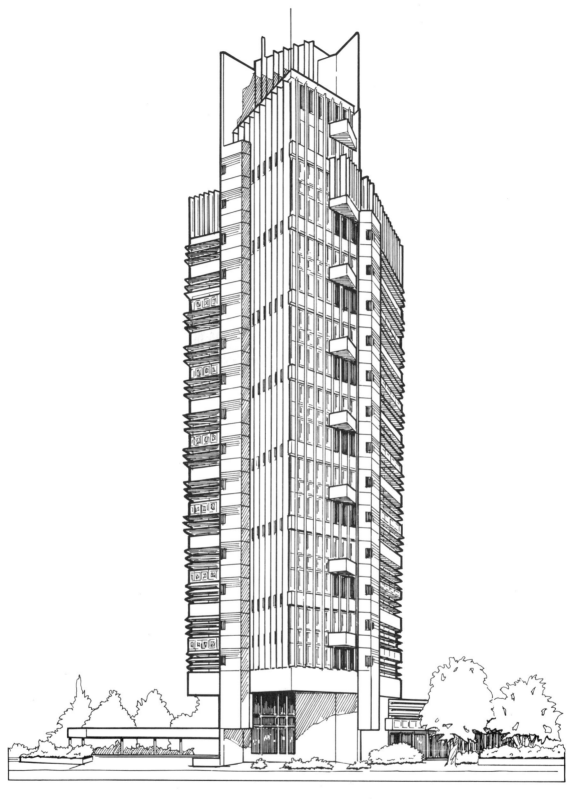

H. C. Price Company Tower (1953–1956), Bartlesville, Oklahoma.

"This skyscraper, planned to stand free in an open park and thus be more fit for human occupancy, is as organic as steel in tension and concrete in compression can make it." — FLLW   The 19-story Price Tower was Wright's only skyscraper design to be built. Directly traceable to his earlier plan for the St. Mark's Tower in New York City, the building rises up from the dusty plains of Bartlesville, Oklahoma, a small city just north of Tulsa.

The Price Tower follows Wright's idea for a building featuring a steel-core center shaft with concrete floor slabs cantilevered out at each level, much like branches from a tree. The concrete slabs are significantly thicker where they meet the shaft than they are at the outside of the building. Glass and copper cover and decorate the outer surface of the building.

Wright felt strongly that skyscrapers should not be built grouped together so as to form dark, sunless canyons of concrete and steel, but rather should stand alone in parklike settings. This would allow the buildings to be more approachable on a human scale, as well as enable them to be viewed more completely.

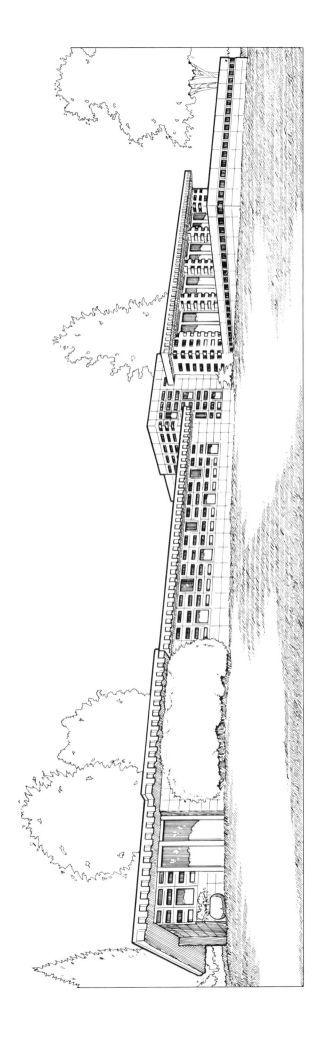

Gerald B. Tonkens Residence (1954), Amberley Village, Ohio. The Tonkens house, the last of Wright's residential designs to be constructed out of concrete blocks, was built when the architect was 87 years old. It was designed as a modified and extended Usonian-house plan and built of ready-made modular units.

The concrete blocks are decorated with patterns and perforations, and steel reinforcing rods are set into the mortar between each two courses for structural strength. As with Wright's earlier designs, some of the perforated blocks are filled with colored glass to enliven the light-gray concrete surface.

The interior walls and furnishings are built of mahogany, with a portion of the ceiling made of concrete blocks gilded with gold leaf. Although Wright visited the site numerous times, the actual construction was supervised by his grandson Eric Lloyd Wright.

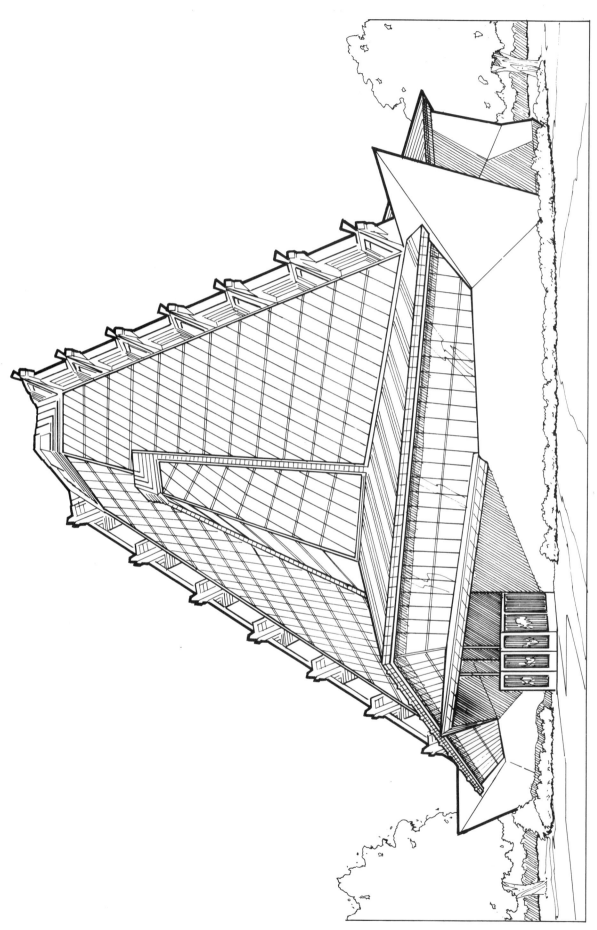

Beth Sholom Synagogue (1953–1959), Elkins Park, Pennsylvania. *"I wanted to create the kind of building that people, upon entering it, will feel as if they were resting in the hands of God."* —FLLW   Among the great religious structures that Wright designed late in life is the Beth Sholom Synagogue, built in the Philadelphia suburb of Elkins Park. Its powerful visual concept is loosely based on a stylized representation of Mt. Sinai, the Biblical mountain of God and Moses. In reality, this man-made version is a "Temple of Light." The tripod-shaped structural beams support a vast roof made of glass and translucent plastic, which allows a soft, diffused external light to fill the main worship area. The support structures themselves are made from copper "shells" filled with steel-reinforced concrete. The numerous emblems and design motifs incorporated into the synagogue are based upon images from the Torah (the first five books of the Old Testament).

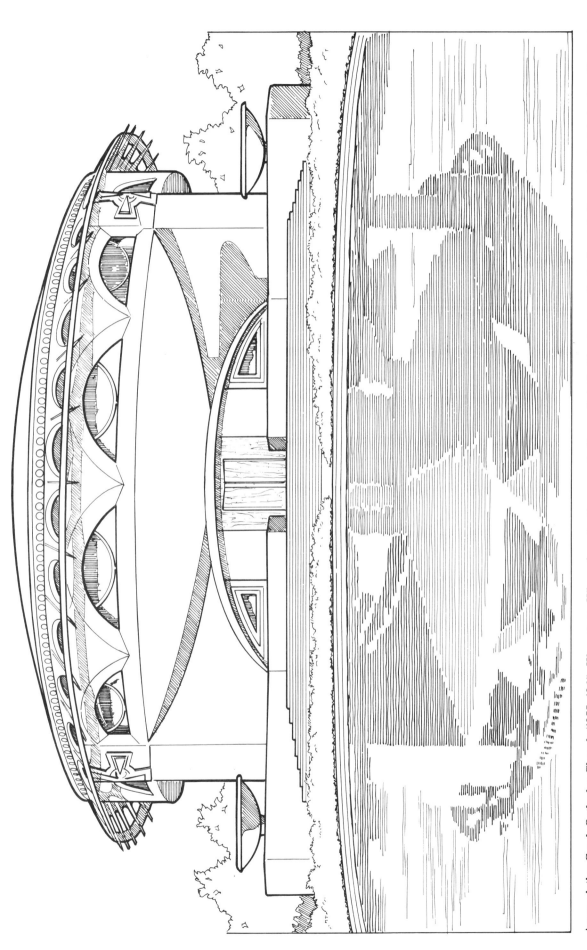

Annunciation Greek Orthodox Church (1955–1961), Wauwatosa, Wisconsin. Another significant religious building designed by Wright in his later years is the beautiful and inspiring Annunciation Church, built for the Greek Orthodox congregation in the Milwaukee suburb of Wauwatosa.

The Greek Orthodox religion represents one of two distinct facets of catholic Christianity. Its roots are found in the Byzantine culture of Asia Minor, rather than in the Western Europe of the Roman Catholic Church. Accordingly, the symbolism and style of design found in Greek Orthodox churches differ greatly from those found in their Western cousins.

Wright's design for the Annunciation Church reflects this Eastern tradition. The repeating arches and the great domed roof of the structure are common elements in Byzantine religious architecture; the building's four supporting columns form the shape of the Greek cross that is used as an ornament on the concrete walls outside.

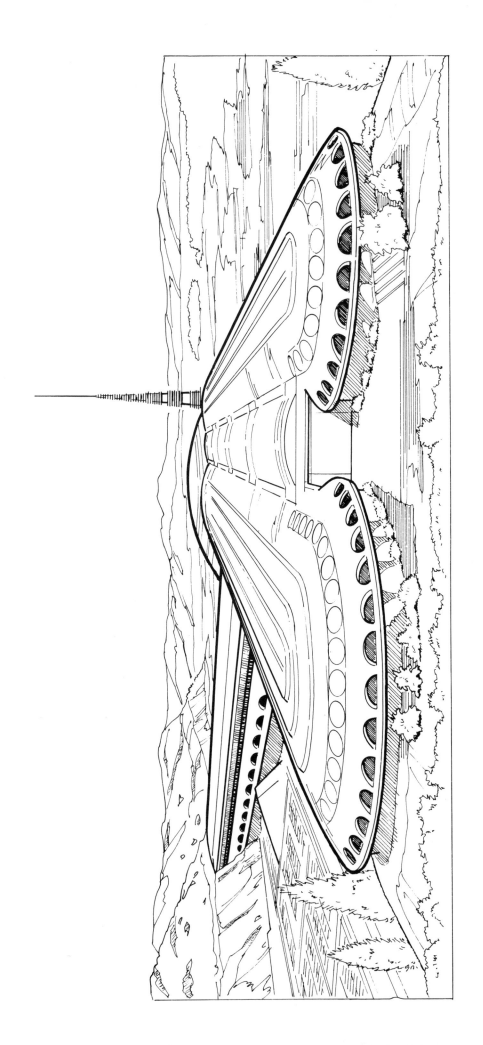

Marin County Civic Center (1957–1961), San Rafael, California. *"Nature is a good teacher. I am a child of hers, and apart from her precepts, cannot flourish. I cannot work as well as she, perhaps, but at least can shape my work to sympathize with what seems beautiful to me in her."* —FLLW   Wright again used the arch and the dome as design elements in the Marin County Civic Center. The plan joins two long wings to a central domed building and its adjacent tower. The concrete wings—supported by a series of multilevel arches—reach from one hill to another, crossing a small valley area much as a bridge spans an open waterway. The wings contain the Marin County offices and Hall of Justice, while the saucer encloses the Public Library. Running the length of both wings is a central mall area with a blue, plastic-domed skylight. All of the offices within the buildings have a view of either the central garden mall or the hills outside.

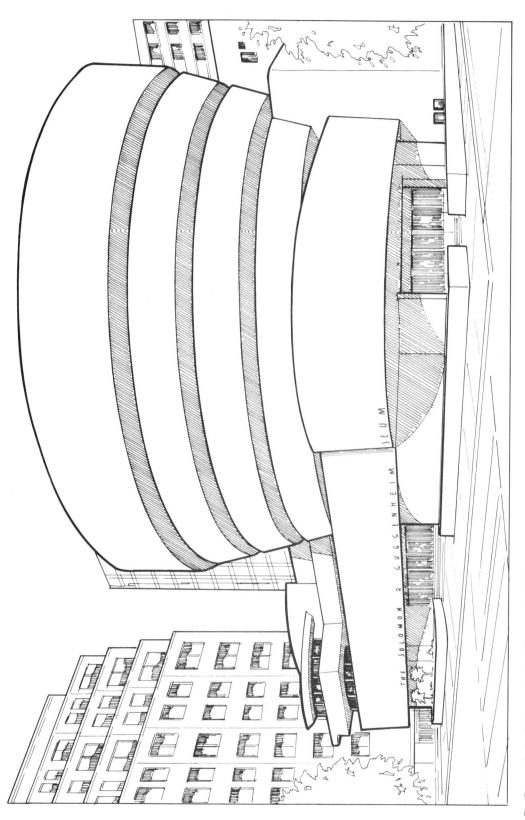

THE SOLOMON R. GUGGENHEIM MUSEUM

Solomon R. Guggenheim Museum (1943–1959), New York, New York. *"It is not to subjugate the paintings to the building that I have conceived this plan. On the contrary, it was to make the building and the paintings an uninterrupted, beautiful symphony such as never existed in the World of Art before."*—FLLW   One of Frank Lloyd Wright's most admired and recognizable architectural works is the Guggenheim Museum in New York City. Conceived and built over a span of 16 years, it was finally opened to the public in October 1959, six months after the death of its architect.

The plan is based on the idea of a ramp spiraling ever upward. Wright's concept was that museum-goers would enter the building, take an elevator directly to the top of the ramp, and then make their way back down at a leisurely pace past the paintings on exhibit. The interior walls of the ramp are sloped slightly backward as if to suggest that the paintings are mounted on an artist's easel.

The artwork in the museum includes the sizable painting collection of the wealthy art patron Solomon R. Guggenheim. It represents the modern "nonobjective" school of painting, with the work of artists such as Picasso, Kandinsky, Klee, Léger and Chagall on exhibit. Both Wright and Guggenheim shared the common goal of creating a museum environment that would be as revolutionary as the paintings themselves. Wright succeeded magnificently by shaping steel, concrete and glass into this impressive embodiment of his beloved "organic architecture."